PAINTING 1956 50 7/10 x 63 1/5"
*Private collection*

# SOULAGES

## By Hubert Juin
*Translated by Haakon Chevalier*

*Twelve Color Plates and*
*Black and White Illustrations*

GROVE PRESS, INC. · NEW YORK
EVERGREEN BOOKS, LTD. · LONDON

# INTRODUCTION

In every new painting the world is discovered. History, which can prove anything and finally proves nothing but itself, is incapable of accounting for a certain savor that makes painting precisely what it is: an exercise of poetry. The world, it will be objected, is not new. When Columbus' caravels arrived and moored at the gates of the unknown continent, the world became round once and for all, and its movement that turns it upon itself makes us lose any hope of knowing it better. And yet this old world—which is reality—cannot forever be seen with the same eyes. We ourselves are Heraclitus' river.

And it is because we are the river that history, which has become insatiable, can today claim this sovereignty. I have made the point before: no exact account of painting can be given by explaining its motives. An equally false picture would be created by the opposite approach, if its secret were sought in the painter's whim. No, painting has a meaning, just as it has a savor, just as it exists. It is in this life that it must be caught: a secret life, woven in that language which is itself the captive, no longer of paper and ink, but of the great spaces of the canvas and of the great signs of the hand.

That painting has a meaning seems to me self-evident. I find it hard to understand the painting that seeks its limits in itself, that claims to be fully embodied in the single act of painting, that proclaims aloud that it imposes no obligation. This was how the *Bourgeois Gentilhomme* acted, making prose without being aware of it. All language has a meaning. Beneath the tic of a period is concealed the sense of this period. There is no language that is not encumbered with history, as there is no longer any history when men are mute. Expression and history go together, and, without being reducible to a single term, without being equivalent, unable to wed, go hand in hand, following the same path.

The theories that challenge one another today are theories that reduce: the Marxist will explain the why and the how of a painting, but the painting itself, its coming into being, its intimate nature, will forever elude him; the psychologist will explain the detail, the architecture, the intimacy, even the soul of a painting, but the speech the painting proffers, what it urges upon the world and what the world urges upon it, all this will find no place in his lesson. Of course one must use whatever tools come to hand, choose from among the theories those that complement one another and combine their elements: join to Marxist analysis psychological unveiling, then, when this has all been gathered together, the trap laid, expose oneself at last to the painting, to that more precise and deeper meaning which is its own and which is *poetry*.

It has been said of the painting of our period that it is a liberated, free painting, capable of going in all directions, of streaming in all directions. This is true. It would be "fun" to list minutely, to make the most complete and rigorous inventory possible of what our period has proposed in the field of plastic arts. I say "fun," because it seems that nothing would be so supremely and deliberately useless as such an inventory and such definitions. The painting of our time, in that great moment of folly that accompanied its initial audacities, was not a liberated painting, but quite precisely an exploded painting. Initial audacities? Oh, such timid ones, and how quickly exceeded: it was only necessary to lose the object. Today a new audacity makes its demands and its weight felt: the creation of a style. As we know, it is not speaking that is most important, but ordering speech; it is not singing that is imperative, it is ordering song; it is not painting that is capital today, it is ordering painting. The importance lies in giving meaning. It is not flinching either before the consequences or before the laws of expression.

"Speak yourself to the stones that speak," says the Rig-Veda. We need today the courage to speak to these signs all about us, in other words to hear them in the first place and, above all, to let them speak, to let them utter their truth. It is written in the same hymn of the ancient sacred book:

> These stones speak in one hundred, in one thousand manners, roar with their yellowed mouths.

And it is for us to make silence. For us—and for painters. This man, who before the intact screen is preparing to incarnate the signs, to erect with the brush the steles that will sooner or later be, in some manner, the signs and the steles of our daily life, this man is nothing other, in the pleasure he derives from painting, in the anguish he feels in tarnishing virgin space, than an orderer. It is said that Demosthenes used to fill his mouth with small pebbles to force himself to speak distinctly. What is the good of a stuttering orator? Demosthenes' small pebbles should be dedicated to our modern painters. What, indeed, is the good of an orderer without order!

But creating a style is neither a simple matter nor an easy one. Rigor is needed. An inner disposition decides for or against this rigor. Freedom is needed. Measure is needed—a measure all the bolder as it must, perforce, continually improvise itself. One does not invent language: language is forged in history itself, by a long procession of human beings. But it is sometimes given to certain ones, who are the poets, to create a new order in language, to liberate from this old and dusty language a young lyricism, one never heard before, new. One does not invent painting—neither the triangle, nor the round, nor the line, nor the spot, nor the landscape, nor the portrait. But it is given to certain ones, the true masters, by a certain manner they have of assembling the syllables of their works, to revolutionize both the past and the future.

There are periods that are essentially dominated,

that are devoured by the absence of orderers. Language turns breathlessly on itself. Rhetoric, like "good painting," invades everything. Skill speaks more loudly than justice. Garrulous thinking submerges everything. The world is open, waits, wonders. Ours is such a period: we have pushed language to the end of its course. But language is never at the end of its course, and will never be at the end of its course so long as a man remains to carry it farther. And man can do nothing but carry it farther.

What is conquered is conquered in the order of language. It does not, indeed, suffice to measure oneself with the world, one must order an experience that one has of it. Therefore nothing is more important than style (or organization of lyricism) because style is, of itself alone, the aptness of language.

I

I am writing these words in connection with Pierre Soulages, because this painter and his work offer me a *reality* of painting and initiate me into a *realism*. An exhibition of his work that I saw at the Galerie de France won me over: those canvases revealed both a sense of the *sacred* to which I could not fail to respond and a calm, rooted, wholly earthy solidity. I was not offered an odd architecture, a perpetual invention looped over upon itself. I was made to accept a somber energy, a certainty. This had a meaning, it was organized forcefully, became—at the very first contact—a fundamental attitude and a decisive choice. Soulages obliged me to meditate on the necessity of painting. Whereas other painters captivated me by the succulence of details in their work, this one informed me at the outset that novelty in painting resides less in a formal outer novelty than in the revelation of a combination of necessary relations among all the elements that contribute to a painting and, at the same time, to a *poetic*.

When one goes through the rooms of a museum, one forms an odd idea of painting; in spite of oneself strange associations are made; in short, one finally discovers that there are no inventors in painting. A form is not an invention. One does not choose one type of painting, one is first of all faithful to his conception of the world. One may compare, for example, the head in the lower left-hand section of Picasso's *Guernica* and the head of the corpse in the lower left-hand section of the *Deluge* in Saint-Sever's *Apocalypse*. In the same way, *Guernica*, which conforms to a compositional plan similar to that of the tympanum of Autun, is not really comparable to the tympanum of Autun any more than it is to certain Renaissance paintings that conform to this same pyramidal plan. Only the necessity of form testifies in the artist's favor. And the museum rooms have the advantage of showing, in the procession of works that have sprung from the succession of centuries, that painting is not defined by its mere formal invention, but on the contrary by an inner life—the painter's—which at the same time has totally vanished. What remains is a trace, a note, an accent, which resides in a manner wholly unique to this work of manifesting itself in the order of the visible.

In front of Van Gogh's straw chair there is no great merit in exclaiming, "Well! A chair!" What we have is something quite different: it is, in fact, a conception of the world. Before certain of Soulages' canvases, it would be a mistake to observe: "It reminds me of a factory building or a cathedral." What takes place in the canvas, what is recorded—here beneath the appearance of an object brutally wrenched from the world of utensils, there in the guise of signs cut off from their role of indications—what is recorded is the manner in which the painter faces the world. The creator's freedom consists wholly in this.

Because this expression gives its assent to the world, ventures into the world itself, and becomes defiance, this painting signifies the world. It obeys the same rules as the poem; through the miracle of its language and its order it becomes the response of a man to the challenge held up to him by both the world and destiny. This upsurge in which it might seem captive constitutes, rather, its freedom. It ceases to be continuity, discourse; it is time trapped, saved, a mirror that cannot be denied, a debate in which freedom is committed. Yet the whole power of the painting collapses if it refuses to take upon itself the deep exigency of language. It disappears if, to the world's exuberance, it responds with the exuberance of expression. It is strong only through its economy. It is valid only by virtue of the order which it contains within itself, and which resists disorder. It is unforgettable to the extent to which it is a synthesis, to the extent to which its upsurge, in its characteristic, immobilized impetus, resists the disorder of the world—and of death....

The chair painted by Van Gogh is, through the painting, a challenge to the world in the name of the life of Van Gogh: it is there as an element of the world to be destroyed. In Soulages' painting, the world is not recorded object by object, but passes, in its totality, into the dynamic experience it provides for the painter. Through his works he proposes to the spectator's imagination an experience

PAINTING   1947   25 1/2 x 19 1/2"
*Private collection*

of the world with which the latter can compare his own. The world here is met in its totality and no longer term by term. No object is elected. If this painting ceases to be a synthesis, it ceases to signify the world. It has no alternative: either it signifies the totality of the world, or it disappears. Here is where the ultimate rigor of Soulages' experience reveals itself.

By the same token, painting is a poetic experience. Its language is related to lyricism, and only poetry is capable of ensnaring time. And because it is a poetic experience, painting will not signify the world in its disorder. It will pick up the challenge by transfiguring the totality of the world. Its response is a metaphor. Its language is a transfiguration.

On museum walls the painting is nothing so long as eyes do not come to awaken it. It is the spectator who gives it its final meaning. For the fundamental freedom of the painter is matched by the fundamental freedom of the spectator. The painting is between them, a marvelous matter that one must ceaselessly take unaware; a trapped moment that must be liberated each moment; a response whose syllables must be made to ring out endlessly; a captive poem of the materials; mingled rhythm and space, a fusion of forms and colors, which nail it to the wall and which must be delivered again and again.

In esthetics theories follow one upon another. We are not yet delivered from Plato. But at the moment when the theory of ideal beauty pre-existing in the zenith of a heaven peopled by unclad forms (unclad and already fallen, being imagined, as the habit is, deprived of roots) appears to strip art of its savor, the seductions of disharmony and of the arts that ignore the golden number are discovered. It suffices neither to account for what motivates a painting in order to account for the painting, nor to translate the composition of a work into mathematical formulas for this work to live again. It is by art that man bears witness. And it suffices to strip a work of this essential testimony to kill it immediately.

Forms respond to one another. The too-small heads of the wonderful bronzes of Pompeii match the too-long arm of Cézanne's *Young Man with the Red Vest*. The Cycladic idols, from the margins of history, match the eyeless faces of the history that has been in process through modern sculpture. It is not primarily the same manner of seeing the world, it is primarily a necessity to defend in art the testimony of man; to maintain the disquieting necessity of art. Who is free in the socialist realism of Fougeron and of Guerassimov? Neither the painter nor the spectator. What would one propose to him who proposes nothing to you? By what could the spectator answer to that which answers nothing? Art is that by which the real proposes itself, it being impossible for the real ever to appear save through and in the language of men.

It has often been said, and, incidentally, in connection with certain drawings and paintings of 1948 and 1949 by Soulages, that Chinese writing has a revival in the signs of our moderns. At a point in his development Soulages was led to break with graphic expressionism. He no longer wanted the lines he drew to guide the spectator and cause him, through the movements that were

PAINTING   1948   45 1/5 x 31 1/5"
*Private collection*

those of the painter's hand, to relive a certain soul-state. He organized these lines—which, let us note, elude the pure writing of movement: they are irreplaceable to the extent to which their existence is woven of a space, a vibration, a density, which are personal. He incarnated them in a great sign, which refused the spectator the facility of the path: the eye embraces the sign, in a single moment, in its totality. Through this conception of the work of art—resolutely non-expressionist—is revealed an experience of the time. And it is not by chance that the signs drawn between 1947 and 1949 (principally) by Soulages make one think of Chinese writing. What we read in them is not Chinese writing, it is a poetic of the time. In an essay that appeared long ago in *Verve*, Paul Claudel noted:

> *Chinese writing, although I have never studied it sufficiently to be able to interpret it fluently, has always exerted a kind of fascination over me, which I attribute to its intrinsic and, if I may say,* timeless *immobility, altogether different from the persistent furrow that this metallic point between the fingers of our personality in the path of explanation leaves behind it. When, in writing* It is three o'clock, *my pen reaches the end of the sentence, it is already no longer three o'clock. But the three strokes of the Chinese brush suffice to record this brief moment in the substance of eternity. Not only is it three o'clock, but each time that a human eye attaches itself to this intellectual nodus, it will never cease to be three o'clock. Among all the characters that form the page, of paper, of bronze, of granite, proposed for my attention, there is no longer a succession,*

*there is simultaneity. There is no longer sound, there is idea. There is no longer a current, an uninterrupted link of discourse resulting from all the articulations and inflections of sonority and syntax, there is a series of isolated notions among which our eye and our intelligence are left to establish relations. When I write* I am going to the house, *using my pen in the same manner as my legs, I repeat in brief the act that leads me to it and that continues to carry the reader along. But the Chinese, with a few delicate black hairs, confines himself to lifting to the dignity of figures three somewhat impersonal concepts: I—to go—house. It is up to the reader, after the writer, to transform into movement what was mere juxtaposition. There is the evocation of a fact, there is no longer communication with an act. There is no longer a succession, there is an emanation of relationships.*

Between Chinese writing and the signs drawn by Soulages there is, not an influence, but an encounter. Despite the differences that separate Soulages' poetic and Chinese writing, it is interesting to point out how a temporal experience can have determined a formal coincidence of this kind.

When the sign ceases to be writing, when it is no longer called upon to record in the very fabric of eternity *it is three o'clock,* when on the contrary it is a matter of involving the sign (or, more accurately, form) in the world by signifying the thread to the labyrinth. Soulages' sign is not a labyrinth: it stands erect. There is in it a verticality that saves it from detours. It is hieratic and *given*. If one is willing to see it one cannot forget it. But what one sees in it, first of all, is the metaphor that nothing can eat into, the enigma that it is. If one cannot recompose it as metaphor, one can nevertheless attempt a formal analysis of it, and explore its syntax. The deep reality of the work will escape us: one cannot put freedom into a formula. The content is linked to the form, but to analyze the form is still not communicating with the work. To explore this syntax is to make an accounting with the means. This is an aspect that must not be neglected.

This painting by Soulages is given all at once. There is a group of lines combining to form a sign, the whole dominated by the vertical. The sign is composed of a series of contrasts: curved lines and angular lines; vertical lines and horizontal lines; movements toward the right and movements toward the left. Let us note that Soulages' lines refuse elegance and glibness, which generally manifest themselves by inflection: they are direct, sober, and avowed. The virtual oblique that can be clearly perceived in the upper part of the sign and which repeats the oblique at the bottom exalts, because it is interrupted, the vertical lines. The dynamism of these, moreover, is intensified by their curved beginning. Because they are assembled into a single sign, these lines determine different surfaces of unequal values. The very quality of the background is modified by the architecture of the contrasts. This background becomes a constructive element of the sign, without the necessity for Soulages to work it out: the lines alone, by their contrasts, awaken it and animate it.

Thus, by the quality of the strokes, by a combination of contrasts, by values pictorially attributed to surfaces, the sign finally surges up into a single vertical thrust that offers it to the spectator in a sudden fling. And it is in this fling that the metaphoric reality of the sign becomes incarnated. Thus, this sign is the experience of the world, and because my glance seizes it, the world is concerned. Soulages early gave up the pleasure of the curve, of the hand gliding at will along the proffered surface.

Poetry here is caught in the snare. How could it be otherwise? But the snares in which it is caught are no longer those of harmony and of complicity. The poetry will be discovered in the broad stroke that testifies, by the fringes that border it, by its paint quality, by its direction, that a sovereign hand was lifted at such a point.

But a painting is not in the stroke: it is in the organization of relations and contrasts that sometimes unite, sometimes oppose the strokes, the surfaces, the spaces, the colors, the lights, the opacities, the transparencies.... The poetry of a pictorial work is read in that structure peculiarly its own, by which all these elements achieve their full coherence. Every pictorial work possesses an authentic and unique coherence. This coherence is the true pictorial language. There is a language

PAINTING   1953   76 x 50 7/10"
*Private collection*

that is Soulages', a pictorial *totality* that is personal to him. It is to the elements of this language, to the analysis of this coherence, that we must give our attention now. The architecture of this painting (of February 1948) introduces us to the very complexity of the means and the elements of Soulages' expression.

Soulages never allows color to have its own way: he does not think in terms of color alone. His austerity before the aggressiveness of colors is neither a lack nor a refusal, but the sign of a deep search and a conviction. Color is never pushed to its full sensorial intensity. It is restrained. The reds and the yellows tend toward ochre. The blues are nocturnal blues. The colors acquire their brightness from the blacks next to them. In this work dominated by black, this black color is strangely and infinitely varied, by virtue of the specificity, of the solidity (well-nigh hieratic) of the pictorial structure, as well as by the contrasts and the relations that are woven, in Soulages' canvas, among the various elements.

In short, the painter makes a choice in favor of poetic intensity alone. He elects the secrets of poetry. The relations with color maintained by the painter define a poetic, but this poetic itself can be approached only by taking into account the economy and the sobriety of the line, of the form, and of the structure.

This color is proposed: it has been lived by the painter, it must be re-created by the spectator. If Soulages happens, in a given painting, to name a color (a bright red, white, blue) at a precise point,

24

it is because the stridency thus solicited will have the immediate effect, by contrast, of thrusting the rest of the picture into a universe of secret, even nocturnal, relations.

Rarely are harmonies found in Soulages' work: the shades generally accompany one dominant and thus enable violent contrasts of values and directions to stress the breaks in space that characterize the work. Color becomes poetic intensity. It becomes rhythm. But this violence and this rhythm, as I have said, refuse the inflections, the sentimentality, or the elegance of the line as well as those of color.

The color is in the form, not superadded to it or conceived independently of the paint-matter, but given at the same time, in a single movement. It is not contained in a contour: it is at the same time surface, matter, and contour.

It cannot be said of Soulages' color that it is poor, any more than it can be said that it is sumptuous. Such terms are inappropriate here. Color is nothing in itself, since it cannot be separated from the matter and the form, like the other elements of the painting. It receives its quality from the coherence of the whole, yet it is essential to the whole; a fundamental choice and attitude.

The painting thus conceived is not an abstraction, it is a metaphor. It is not proposed to the spectator in order to refer him to given concepts to which the work is the key. What saves it from dispersion—and this would be precisely dispersion—is its upsurge. Because it is frozen time it does not allow itself to be decomposed by reasonable speculations. It is an upflung metaphor, having its source in the very depth of a being, but abolishing, in the selfsame moment of its emergence, that depth of being: the work proceeds *from* the intimate substance of the painter, and no sooner does it exist than it denies, at the very outset, the painter's intimate substance. It begins to exist in the objective universe, itself an object, and at the same time not reducible to the order of objects. If its bursting-forth, its essentially abrupt nature saves it from men, its quality of metaphor, its connivance with poetry saves it from the world of objects. It occupies an intermediary rank, responding equally well, and with the same violence, to the former and to the latter. It is alone in possessing the greatest of privileges, the privilege of involving, in its very upsurge, in the mere fact of its being (and of being for *nothing*), all the freedoms offered before it, all the freedoms confronting it. Singular indeed is its dialectic: it is for *nothing,* and if one but contemplate it, it becomes at once for *all.*

It is an image of the world, but also a manner of thinking. It could not be that metaphoric image (that image to which the poem alone, in the verbal order, brings a response), without at the same time being that singular idea.

I have before my eyes this great sign of Soulages', which piles up black forms, establishes them in verticality, embraces them in a single rhythm pressing upward (two white flashes further stressing the essential architecture): how has it been thought out?

PAINTING  1957  50 7/10 x 63 1/5"
*Private collection*

I believe that the plastic arts achieve, before the verbal arts do, a necessary conversion.

We have waged a hard battle to conquer reason, but in conquering reason it is not reason alone that we have finally possessed; the whole struggle that we have had to wage over the centuries to conquer it fairly holds us captive today. We have conquered reason in the hope of de-mythifying the world. But the movement that we have created to conquer reason has, in exactly the same measure, re-mythified the world.

In this combat human expression has become an intentional expression. With every imagined story went a "moral." What shocked the public when Manet showed *Olympia* was the absence of intentions. The contingency of objects and of the world was denied, because reason in order to be conquered requires objects and the world to have a meaning. But in doing this we excluded ourselves from a communion with the world, a communion found intact, however, in "Negro" thinking. We have denied ourselves participation.

If, in the modern novel, our good writers endeavor to omit all intention, this procedure still remains a procedure of the mind, still belongs in the order of intention. Painters—or so it seems—are privileged in this respect. I see no *intentions* in Soulages' canvases, but at the same time I do not think that this lack of *intentions* is itself an intention. This is worth observing: there cannot be intentions in an upsurging and in the reign of the abrupt. The sign before my eyes eludes the realm of concepts. It is a metaphor to which we must always return, as well as to poetry. Its order is an immediate order, altogether similar in *nature* to the immediate disorder of the world. This is why, too, it takes up the challenge held up to it by the world, this is why it is a response, and this is why, similarly, man's greatness lies in this response. Man's greatness, but not man himself, who is immediately rejected by the work, who is obliged, in the exile in which the work ceaselessly stalks him, forever to begin again, and, as Focillon says, to *begin again the same search*. In the old sacred book of India are to be found some very instructive lines:

> The Orderer has given shape
> to the Sun and the Moon, in the first rank;
> to Heaven and Earth;
> to airy Space; and finally to Light.

But where is the Orderer himself, if not in this act by which he gives shape, if not in exile?

So it is with the poet: in this library, which erects its ramparts of bindings around him, he is the god who gives shape. Let him but seize a book, no matter what book, and this book becomes animate, alive. But if the poet takes his own book and opens it, he will only seize a dead matter. And this exile in which he thus finds himself will oblige him, in the silence of his room, once again to attempt the impossible.

There was a good deal of Prometheism in a certain idea of the "esthetically perfect" pursued by certain painters: they were aiming at nothing less than accomplishing painting and rendering it henceforth impossible. It is an illusion. But such illusions are undoubtedly necessary, enabling men to push farther forward.

In Soulages' explorations—after a period in which the forms invited and required the eye of the spectator to come and bring them together, not at his will, but according to a very strict pattern that alienated this fundamental freedom—we have witnessed a series of great canvases in which the forms, in their upsurging, refuse succession. They are simultaneous. The spectator's eye can unite them, and this indeed is what he does, but he is wholly free of this union. The union, moreover, in no way alienates the simultaneity of forms. Everything is given in the same instant without an instant, at the same time rescued from time but springing from time.

And the movement that one sees in Soulages' paintings (one might, to be sure, believe that in this abrupt upsurging, in this simultaneity all movement must disappear) is exactly and uniquely linked to the movements of freedom.

Not only the moment is ensnared in Soulages' work. There is also—through a succession of constants, such as verticality, the suggestion of color, etc.—an implicit dynamism. It is never *represented,* and yet it is everywhere visible. It is not exactly suggested, which would impair the abrupt character of the work. It is caught in its entirety in the pictorial matter, in the same manner as the ideas of elevation, of upward thrust, of sovereign verticality are caught in the folds of stone of cathedrals or certain rocky figures created by erosion and the race of time.

Before Soulages' work, the spectator is not invited to *see*, to observe the dynamism; he is rather commanded by this dynamism: he *experiences* it. Here we must beware of words: dynamism does not mean movement. Soulages does not describe a movement. For that matter, a painting that describes a movement, that proposes the traces of a preconceived movement, does not thereby become a dynamic painting. Soulages' canvas, however, imposes its energy on the spectator. This energy is not dependent upon a description, an account of movements, but upon a combination of pictorial qualities, a language.

We shall likewise discover in Soulages' works a rhythm that is their own. The forms pile up according to a rhythm that is not represented, not suggested, but captive to that black color that has become a prime and dominant color for our painter.

There is no Platonic paradise of forms because, pictorially, form does not exist: it cannot be isolated, it too is caught, as in the folds of rock, in the snares of color and of matter. The painting is a *material* upsurge. The concept cannot cling to this solid architecture. But the idea captive to this mastery of the hand saves us from the domestications of reason. Through it, we come upon the world.

And thus we find ourselves, through the work, and before the work, in singular relationships: this painting that piles up its black forms is for us a witness to an experience of the world in the experience of poetry; this painting is for us a closed area in which our metaphor is measured by a metaphor that is proposed to us; this painting is for us an opening through which we suspect that the real is not wholly this formula, this myth to which centuries would like to reduce it.

An affirmation held up to the affirmation of the world, an order challenging disorder, that is the pictorial sign. After which: an opening through the virtues and the apanage of poetry upon the freedom of the world and the freedom of the elements. Finally: a higher organization by which language itself becomes organized....

Painting must be restored to its meaning. Because it escapes every analysis reduced to the search for and the accomplishment of the motivations presiding over its genesis; because an analysis limited to the presence of the painter in his work and an analysis that aims at being mathematical and believes in the Platonic paradise show themselves successively to be incapable of accounting for the very meaning of the work, it was thought necessary to abandon painting to painting, to see in it a "doing," to follow the sheer ambitions of the hand. This is an error. Painting is a human expression. By virtue of this, it concerns man. It is a free activity. By virtue of this, it involves freedom. It is situated in the world. By virtue of this, it participates in the universe.

# II

Among the works of modern painting, it is Soulages' canvases that give to the greatest degree the sensation of the *sacred*. As though the work proposed to us maintained with the universe essential relations that intimately concern us. And, in truth, as we have seen, this work does maintain with the universe relations of totality. Certain critics have sought to read religious overtones into this work; for one, the crucifixion, and the implicit presence of salvation through suffering; for another, the painter's night quivering with the presence of the hidden God. I share neither of these views. Explaining this diffuse sensation amounts to grappling with the very intimacy of this pictorial art; it is seeking to go beyond the analysis of the appearances of this work toward the conception of the world linked to a work which is to an exemplary degree free of intentions. It is therefore the crucial point of the analysis. It amounts to attempting to develop the *meanings* of the work from what we know of the *bearing* of the work. And this development, this analysis, cannot be attempted in language other than through a series of metaphors. In order to enter into the painter's secret, one must necessarily cease to navigate in close proximity to the *matter* that he presents to us. I shall have occasion to come back to this, but a commentary is nothing more than an open passage in a language which is not that of the creator himself. How to open this passage, if not by way of metaphor?

Soulages tends to resent religious interpretations of his paintings. This is a reference of prime importance....

The time of the work is not the time of everyday life; the space of the work is not the space of everyday life, it is more essential than this everyday space and it introduces in us a dramatization of space. Let us look a little more closely: going from the Galeries du Commerce to the Café de la Paix in our innumerable towns is an act accomplished by innumerable men every day. Painting (this painting) introduces a dramatization of space by unveiling the dynamism within it. Literally, from this slant, the space separating the Galeries from the Café becomes a drama of daily life, loses its blind character, becomes illuminated, and man, the spectator, is caught up by the dramatic implications.... It is in this sense (and it is only slightly, for reasons of clarity, that I strain my images a little!) that the work makes a turn-about to everyday life, challenges it, illuminates it, is unwilling to be isolated from it. On the contrary: it draws this life upward. It presents itself to this life as an exemplarily assumed life!...

Even as painting, by its very existence, possesses a meaning, in the same manner, insofar as it is an event in the world, it is endowed with an exemplary moral quality (in short, it is that by which

PAINTING 1957 14 4/5 x 21 1/2"
Collection Galerie de France, Paris

a man, as a splendid outcast, has lived exemplarily the dimensions of man in the world). Not that it is lawful or baneful in this precise case, that it leans toward good or evil, but that it will, in its dynamism and by the verticality in it, enable man to discover his freedom, and the spectator his commitment.

Painting is neither a setting nor an ornament. It refuses to limit itself to esthetics alone. The esthetics it claims is of another kind, more rigorous, less confined: it does not aim at pure beauty, for it does not leave the world intact. It admits esthetics to the extent to which the organization of language, the organization of lyricism, is its *necessary* condition. But it refuses an esthetics that becomes sheer charm and ceases to be a precise language. Immortality or the tribute of posterity will be given it for good measure. I am reminded in this connection (in connection with the "work") of the splendid line by a Greek poet—by the Greek poet, to be exact, who went so far in the quest of lyricism as to designate Medusa's head "death of stone," Pindar:

> *O my soul, do not aspire to immortal life, but exhaust the field of action that is given to you...*

and this line is like the mute exhortation that the true artist addresses to his own language!

Let us come back to the work (and let us not lose sight of Soulages' work in these remarks of general import): through it freedom is discovered,

PAINTING   1957   76 x 50 7/10"
*Collection Kootz Gallery, New York*

but through it too freedom discovers itself to be vain. The delivered painter begins again, and still begins again. The solicited spectator reads in the work his own links with the world.

To be condemned to freedom, as a contemporary philosopher puts it, is nothing other than to reduce freedom to absurdity, than to acquiesce in a freedom without vocation. For, when freedom is *for nothing*, it is no longer freedom; it has lost the sense of challenge: it no longer rebels, it no longer responds to that which, in the world, in destiny, shocks it and shocks man. All true freedom is both a question and an answer, a tragic question and an anguished answer. To freedom alone is given the power to awaken drama in the heart of the numbness of the everyday. To freedom alone is given the power to deny the aging of the world in man. No freedom, however, can do without the world. No freedom exists if it has not in it a weight that roots it to the ground and an urge that draws it upward.

What has been taken for liberated painting in this century is nothing other than this: a painting that took uprooting for freedom. People painted sentiments, pure (or pretty) painting, or theories (theories are easy to paint). Only recently have we again seen a true painting, truly free to the extent to which this same painting is deeply committed (the word "commitment" is being used in relation to "duel") in the very dialectics of freedom. This goes back to the question of generations.

Soulages is a man of thirty-eight. He belongs to a *rooted* generation, to a generation that does not

PAINTING   1956   31 3/5 x 23 2/5"
*Private collection*

ask where the paths of freedom lie, because these paths and this freedom are given him at the same time that his commitment is given him. This generation rediscovers the earthy solidities that were so lacking in the generation previously sacrificed and dissipated. For this generation there is no lyricism without organization of language, no poetic without a will to order, no work that is not a response, no beauty that is gratuitous, no truth that is not human.

This state surely cannot be achieved without search: this generation, let us not forget, was born in uprootedness, in the bastardy of the preceding one. Every one of the members of this generation had to line up his account of errors, had to come back finally, after the egregious romanticisms, the discredited surrealisms, the weary revolts, toward certain essential affirmations, most of them having to do with the reign of the visible world.

Here, without descending into the "day-to-day" of experience, we can follow Pierre Soulages' experience. What can be expected of this unwonted re-creation? A clarification of the work itself? Hardly. This is a habit left to fanciers of the anecdotal. All we can do is to approach an attitude, and by this attitude illuminate the painter's "present." It would be idle to expect more.

When Soulages had carried out an experiment similar to the one that I shall presently attribute to him in the form of a metaphor (for in this realm only an *as if* is possible), he came to Paris. Must I explain? Very well! I think that he had in his heart the unforgettable archetype that he was to rediscover later....

He came to Paris, almost enrolled in the Ecole des Beaux-Arts, yet did not set foot in it—an exhibition of Cézanne and another of Picasso that he saw awakened in his soul an irresistible calling. He saw other exhibitions and immediately after the war declared himself to be fiercely opposed (and rightly so) to the abstract formalism in vogue at the time. He had something to say: he had no idea what it was nor how to say it. One fall day, as he was walking aimlessly along the banks of the Seine (and I believe everything about this is important: there is a climate of the Seine that is unforgettable and inimitable—did not this landscape create the French language?...) he saw a metal propeller lying on the grease-smeared deck of a barge. This spiral, enclosed in a steel movement against all that *solid*, rich, gritty, dense black, evoked something deep within him: something that was about to be born.... In short, the movement, imprisoned by the blades of the propeller, took hold of him. The splashed grease was proof to him of a rugged reality *to be embraced*. In his studio he made curves, letting his arm and his hand soar freely. He became enchanted, then grew intrigued by the very quality of this enchantment. Upon reflection, there was about it nothing that was not strange. He next tried himself out with forms. He began to order curves, to add to one form already obtained another form, then another, then still another....

This was also an unsatisfying experiment: the

value of the painting could only be measured by an esthetic judgment. When at last, by dint of patient seeking, he succeeded in communicating to his work his own certain poetic experience of the world, he perceived that he was robbing the spectator of his fundamental freedom.

(But all this will already have been guessed, from the preceding part....)

The spectator was obliged to follow the painter; the work was not the desired upsurge, but an itinerary to be followed; it was not the reality to be embraced, but the survey of this reality. To this extent it let itself be exhausted too quickly and too easily by the spectator who, carried along by the painter's still visible hand, did not commit himself, did not commit his deep freedom.

This was indeed the propeller and the spot of tar, not in their resemblance, to be sure, but in this image that has nothing in common with its own model. Yet it was still responding term by term to the elements of the world's totality. In other words, it was not yet responding to the world, it was not yet signifying the world. It was a painting which, although no longer figurative, was not yet pictorial *realism*....

It was when, having passed through these experiences, a more ancient experience returned to take up its sovereign abode in Pierre Soulages, and with it the archetype of verticality, the implicit dynamism, that the work assumed its true character, its present character, and became an upsurge, a response to the world and to destiny. The sign aims to be the synthesis of a vision of

PAINTING   1957   76 x 50 7/10"
*Private collection*

the world. In it is involved the painter's freedom. In it must be involved the spectator's freedom. Its origin is a poetic. Its end is a commitment.

But what about this first experience? How is one to transcribe it? And what could the painter himself tell me about it? I am free—but free *solely*— to re-create it through words, to project it into a realm not naturally its own, to confront it with overtones that are in me, in the depths of my being. Who can say if it is really a question of overtones? Speaking of Soulages' painting in terms of meanings, it is up to me to run the risk of transposing in terms of the written language an experiment that he carried out in his most intimate being. The pages that follow should be regarded as a fable, they should be given the least possible credence. I see no other means of drawing up an agreement of *expression* between Soulages and myself. This book is not intended to be a simple report. To the extent to which it commits me it is obliged to assume itself, and to assume me as well. Once again, here is a fable....

# III

In the countryside at Rodez, the young Soulages began to draw and paint. What challenged him (this is where the fable appears) was the tree. The reasons for this choice that I imagine would be of two orders: external, in the first place, since it would be possible for the young Soulages to deform the tree as he liked without incurring the mockery of his kind, whom he would undoubtedly arouse to frenzy by awkwardly deforming faces. This is a reason of negligible weight. More essentially, there is the fact that this mass, solidly rooted to the ground and lifted upward by an irresistible force, enabled the young man to use the color black. But, deeper yet, other reasons exist, inner ones this time and difficult to formulate: the tree is already the great sign of the freedom of the world.

This verticality, caught in matter as though the very voice of the earth had become immobilized in its vegetal surge, resembles, corrects, approves the stones erected by Celtic Gaul which are seen around the plateaux surrounding Rodez; and resembles, corrects, approves the wonderful relics abandoned there by Romanesque art. The edifice! The Romanesque edifice! It is at once plan and structure, use of space and conception of time, archetypal decision and distribution of masses. It is also—it is above all—a search for architectural unity and a will to nonrationalized meaning. For the Romanesque period, as we see and know, art was never a search for adornment, but humanism, and what is more: humanism of totality, before becoming, in the sumptuous treatises of the philosophers of the end of the Middle Ages, encyclopedic humanism....

In addition to which, who does not know that the tree, in the mute universe, is the image of man?

Every folklore free of Christianity, and thereby free of rationalization, gives recognition to the tree. In Russia, the birch tree is adorned and celebrated. In Australia, in Indochina, in India, in Phoenicia, the tree was identified with the stone, and thus with the altar. It was looked upon as a microcosm. In Mesopotamia, in Scandinavia, the tree was thought to reveal the image of the cosmos. In the Aegean the tree was inhabited, visited by a god.

Its role is considerable everywhere. It is strength, but it is also promise. It is the immutable, but it is also the token of resurrection. It stands erect, and in the movement that lifts it upward, that offers it to a marriage with the stone and with the wind, that tempts lightning and the heavens' wrath, peoples have ever seen an image of man, and through this wonderful image, the symbol of the world's freedom. The tree is the handwriting of nature. It unites the earth with the celestial vault. He who rests at its feet sees how the stars are caught in its leaves. He who stands in its shade

PAINTING 1954 76 x 50 7/10"
*Private collection*

sees how the sun flings its rays on it: hawks of light come and pierce its night.

The Egyptians had made it the Tree of Life, and its branches the generous arms of the divinities. In the Bible it has two aspects: the tree of good and the tree of evil. But it is first of all the very sign of knowledge. From the primitive arts to abstract art, the tree is present, and in no period does it fail to play a privileged role.

We find a good example of this in the work of Mondrian. From *Blue Tree* of 1911 to *The Tree*, also of 1911 and which is in Blaricum, an attempt to geometrize the tree is clearly seen. Mondrian here does not try to stylize the tree, but he draws up its plan, its "survey," if one prefers. He respects its volumes and its master lines. He gives first place, however, not to the verticality of the tree, not to what relates the tree to the stone and to man, but rather to what extends it in space, to what in the tree is in the sense of the wind, to its spreading, in short to what is lateral movement and not an arrested thrust. Two other trials, *Apple Tree in Bloom* (one in The Hague and one in Domburg), show how Mondrian passed from the geometry of the tree to a two-dimensional drawing in which only the scattered elements of the first tree can still be read. If we compare these trials to certain *Compositions* (that of 1913, for example), the tree in its exploded structure will be seen to preside over all this rigor.

This example is interesting to the extent to which it is exactly contrary to Soulages' experience (in the fable, to be sure, but also, I believe, in reality).

PAINTING 1957 23 2/5 x 31 3/5"
Collection Galerie de France, Paris

For the latter, the tree is primarily verticality. Its resemblance to the up-ended stone captivates our painter. And in making an archetype of this verticality he comes back to man. (Beyond this fable that I dedicate to him, it will be recognized that this very notion of verticality must be combined with the use of lateral rhythms of which examples are frequent in Soulages' work.) The tree, in the terrestrial kingdom, is the upsurge. What makes it resemble man is the dynamism that is hidden in it (its heart), that is implicit and yet everywhere perceptible, everywhere present. It is said, in the Rig-Veda, that

> Man has a thousand heads,
> he has a thousand eyes, a thousand feet.
> Covering the earth from end to end,
> he still outmeasures it by ten fingers.

This verticality—for example, the way the cypress flings itself into the blue of the sky—is common to the tree, to the stone, to man.
But it is likewise common, in this sense, to everything that registers in black on the horizon. In the sun, the tree is not green; it is black. Let the wind rise and the olive tree that spots the density of the air with ink will turn up its silver leaves. The erect stone is black when it stands against the sky. Yet let the sun caress its sharpest edges and it will cause a white wound to shimmer curiously. It is in the heart of what is black that what is light appears with the greatest density and the greatest meaning.
And in the same way, Soulages' painting, which

is above all—historically as well as esthetically—the revelation of black as a rich and infinitely varied color,* is a majestic revelation of light. In those great signs that he places on our walls, and that are, like the tree, like the upright stone, like a man standing, enigmas, time is caught and illustrated in the same way that it is caught and illustrated in the course of the seasons, in the rhythm of the year ceaselessly recurring and ceaselessly new. The *passages* in these signs that are the poetry of materiality, these black *passages* on black, according to the hours of the day, will liberate the forms, make them slip over one another, unveil them or conceal them, from dawn to dusk, presenting to the eyes each time the same enigmatic and emerging sign, and each time the perfectly *free*, never repeated play of the forms.

In the course of this fable it will be noticed that the manner of perceiving (quite outside of any art criticism), whether the proposed work is valid or not, consists in testing it. Take yourself as an example: in this room, which is your room, you are now harboring a painting. This painting you see again and again day after day. Morning (when you wake up). Noon (in the midst of your worries, of your joys). Evening (in your fatigue or in your contentment). Let time pass. If you continue to *see* the painting with every glance that you cast on it, if each time it holds your essential nature a little in suspense, that painting is valid. Otherwise, take it down!

I like the fact that Soulages (in the fable, but also

*Marcel Brion, *L'Art Abstrait*, Paris: Albin Michel.

in reality) has attached himself to the lessons of the earth. There is in him, first of all, that solidity rooted to the soil, that way of steering close to earthy lessons. Before his canvas he is like the peasant before his field. The same patience is to be found in both. When he stops the course of his hand in the heart of the completed work, his gesture is comparable to the gesture made by the peasant when he spreads out the wheat of his harvest in sheafs. These gestures have meaning only in their continuity, in their repetition.

The fable continues. Soulages' fundamental attitude toward painting is a radically optimistic attitude. It assumes the continuity of painting. It assumes that painting will continue, that is to say that man, the same man, will resume, will recommence the same searching. Exactly as the fundamental attitude of the peasant is contained in the assurance that after him other men will begin the same work over again, will each year take the world again at its birth in order to lead the world to the unfolding of its finest fruit. When the fields are bare, the world is dead. When the seed rests in the furrows, the world is being born. When the canvas is blank, the world is dead. When the canvas receives the sign, the world in its totality awakens, wholly engaged in this response.

Here the fable should invoke Hölderlin, that poet whose somber brightness has anticipated so many things:

> *This is why when Nature seems throughout*
> *a long season to be sleeping*

*In the sky, or amid the plants or peoples,*
*Poets also go into mourning, they appear*
*Abandoned, and yet sense the future,*
*As it is sensed by she who rests.*
*But dawn glimmers! I have seen it break on*
*the peak of my long wait.*
*Ah, may what I love, the sacred, be my say!*
*For she who is older than Time, she*
*Who dominates the gods of the Orient and*
*those of Evening,*
*Nature! today in a crash of arms has*
*awakened...\**

I do not know if this detour has been useful!
The lessons of the earth! My friend Pierre Soulages has inherited patience, and he has gathered
—as well—that major sign of the freedom of the
world: the tree. I want to make myself under-
stood, and I can do so only by escorting with
images, by escorting with an "as if," my own
knowledge, my subjective understanding! Let us
come back to the fable: the tree escapes the patience of the peasant (the world never dies in
him) but during that same time it verifies this patience, it bears witness in behalf of this patience.
Watching, at the limits of the field, it is, as the
Rig-Veda says, a proof that man

*...is the master of the immortal realm because*
*he believes beyond nurture.*

Soulages, if he rediscovers in his painter's gestures the patience of the peasant, and beyond it
the patience of the earth, discovers as well, *in his*

*From the French translation by Gustave Roud.

*act,* the true greatness of man and the indomitable freedom of the universe. And the painter's patience is likewise history. They are both before the virginity of their realms caught in an historic movement. They are in repetition. But when the painter causes the enigmatic sign which engages freedom to emerge on his canvas he remains—he, the man painting, the man working—in repetition, but this sign that he delegates and that takes leave of him, and that banishes his human powers, escapes repetition, discovers itself in its own upsurge, in that instant without an instant that is its own, and unique: it kills repetition, abolishes it, escapes it. The painter will begin again, but the work has nothing to begin again: it is.

It is on this path, ceaselessly followed and so perilous, that at last, but at what price, the sun of Justice is found....

In one of his great books, William Faulkner says that felled trees cry for vengeance. The meaning of the tree in folklore and in rite is obvious: it is through the tree that man participates in the universe. Reason conquered is the cosmic tree cut at its root. The abandoned universe cries for vengeance. In the vertical and dynamic architecture of this painting, the meaning of the tree is to be found, and with it the very meaning of *participation.* Irreducible, the tree joins the engraved sign, the black stele standing in its upsurge, man at last turned back upon himself and rediscovering his full depth, that is to say: the night, the starry night....

Thus ends the fable....

# IV

Thus ends the fable.... It has, I believe, a deep meaning in relation to our painter, but it lacks literal meaning. I think that Soulages, as a young man, did a good deal of looking at trees and stones. I do not think he let himself be invested by them. I am convinced, furthermore, that Soulages is *earthy*, that he is by predilection attuned to the telluric voices of the world, and that he finds support in them. I can hardly see him undertaking disincarnated experiments, going in for "abstract" adventures. He presents in daily life a host of virtues that show him strangely rooted to the soil, to matter. His love of rusty metal, of all substances in which, as he says, "time has been snared"; his deep love of tools, the wholly metallic solidity of knives, scrapers, *utensils* that one holds firmly in the hand and uses with a certain plenitude and a great happiness, all this undoubtedly gives a more real image of him than the fable that I have dedicated to him. But no matter! Beyond this love of solid, rugged matter, a world of meanings appears, of which the procession of Soulages' works is both sign and clothing. It is to these meanings that my fable is addressed....

Soulages is a painter who likes to prepare his colors himself, who takes great care to make up his own media and blends. But all this also goes back to a meaning and in turn distills a meaning: Pierre Soulages' rootedness. He is a man with his feet on the ground, who has received from nature a number of basic lessons and will not forget them. In his obstinacy and in the exemplary continuity of his work, these lessons can be read in the clear.

I was speaking of the archetype of verticality. I confess that it is a convenient and very useful expression. At the same time, it must be corrected and recognized as having a much greater complexity. It would be more accurate to speak of "rhythms." Soulages' painting is a rhythmic, violently rhythmic, painting. Every canvas is solidly constructed (as though knotted) around a rhythm that is both its soul and its architecture. This dynamism, in the succession of paintings, assumes diverse forms. Sometimes it is pure verticality, a great upward thrust, motionless, and at the same time drawing everything to it. At other times it shows itself in a series of more or less parallel and lateral forms. At still other times it shifts the balance, piling up its greatest density in the upper part of the canvas. And then again, abandoning its "totemic" aspect, its rhythmic writing, this dynamism combines—in great, sumptuous architecture—all these ways of manifesting itself. The idea that there is a similarity among Soulages' paintings is both true and false. The similarity lies in a conception of the world that is implicit and always present. The similarity lies in the strictly dynamic quality, in the *will*, in the somber

PAINTING   1958   45 1/5 x 31 3/5″
Collection Galerie de France, Paris

power of these paintings. But here the similarity ends. One need only look at Soulages' works to see how different they are from one another, to what extent each one is unique and speaks only for itself. Each one presents itself as a pictorial totality, as a unique battle, as a unique response. Each one obeys its own secret laws. Each one, in the shifting light, behaves with its own peculiarities. Each one, finally, after all the others, marks an advance, a new effort, a *"plus oultre."* And this that I wrongly called "obstinacy" becomes one of the master keys of Pierre Soulages' work. It is a work that refuses to close in upon itself and to devour itself.

It has been said of Soulages' painting that it is nocturnal painting. This is (once again) both true and false. It is important in these matters to rule out hasty generalizations and snap judgments! If one allows oneself to contemplate a series of works by Soulages, this prodigious gamut of black worked out and used by our painter will inevitably suggest the very idea of night—not, be it noted, of real night, of temporal night, nor yet of the surrealist night haunted by dreams that are, each time, the more or less legible reverse of the events of the day, but of a more essential, more profound night, of a *sacred* night.

In literature, it can be seen that the night, this same essential night, this same sacred night, this Great Night, insists on appearing. Certain writings (still rare) explore this deep night, but use this night that is both mythical and real—more real than the temporal night, but an image of the

PAINTING   1957   50 7/10 x 34 7/10"
Collection Kootz Gallery, New York

night that in no way resembles the temporal night —to bring forth from language and in language a dimension of man, a dimension that, shorn by this night of all intention, is nothing other than the verticality of man, than the implicit dynamism in him, as it is in the tree, drawing him upward. To such an adventure of letters, Soulages' pictorial adventure forms an echo. Although it should be said that the painter goes farther than the writer!

In the same manner that these writings opening to an *hiérophanie,* opening to the Great Night, give rise to an exceptional space, the very place of this *hiérophanie,* which the romantic heroes, the poetic heroes, and the readers (these mythically) must conquer by their march—even so Soulages' painting creates its own space, which, too, is to be conquered: by the sign first of all (by the painter, in the act of painting) and afterwards by sight (by the spectator who contemplates). Soulages admits it, writing:

> *It is not a simple representation of space that one finds, but space lived, tested, felt in a poetic experience...*

It must constantly be remembered that it is through poetic experience that the work is engraved, is recorded. And it is poetic experience alone, in Soulages' canvases, that guarantees the entire, fundamental freedom of the spectator. It is a question of quality (one should add: and also a question of a man of quality). These works are literally *events.* They do not contain the *morali-*

*ties* that distort the expression of man, and that make every work created the element of an endless discourse. Soulages' canvases are not the terms of a discourse: they escape repetition. They are not a re-beginning of anything. They are, each one of them, and each time, an answer that man makes to the world, a commitment of freedom that responds to the world's freedom.

This night in whose heart they are recorded is perhaps, it has been suggested, the night of the German romantics. It has been said that these works come close to Novalis' *Hymns to Night*. I do not think so. Novalis' "Night" is the paradise of symbols, the place of the Mothers, the stronghold of all the archetypes:

> *Like a monarch of Nature, here below, it invites every force to innumerable metamorphoses, endlessly ties and unties unions, its celestial image irradiating each being on earth. And its sole presence reveals the magnificence of the kingdoms of this world.*

There is but one archetype in Soulages (but is this really a suitable term?): it is the somber energy which is the heart of his work, it is the dynamism. This night is not a symbolic night, it is not a place or an ideal state where the keys of destiny might be discovered, it is the sign that a man has risen, has stood erect, leaving to this very act the acceptance of the challenge....

For Soulages' night is not the absence of colors, quite the contrary: the extraordinary palette in which black dominates suggests with admirable freedom and a magnificent richness all the possible colors—by which I mean not the play of colors, not the charm of colors, but the sense and the meaning of colors. In the way Soulages' canvases vary according to the light, the forms slipping over one another, into one another, color ceases to be superadded: it is itself form and matter. It is no longer an esthetic element but becomes involvement in a human experience, in a *poetic* that is the painter's own. In it can be read the singular, strange necessity of art.

*1957*

# BIOGRAPHICAL NOTES

Born December 24th, 1919, in Rodez, France. Along with his studies at the *lycée* in this southern town, he became interested in prehistoric and Romanesque art of which the region affords remarkable examples. He began to paint when he was very young and devoted himself exclusively to painting as soon as he had completed his secondary studies.

Intending to enroll in the Ecole des Beaux-Arts, he went to Paris in 1939. Numerous visits to the Louvre, a Cézanne exhibition, and a Picasso exhibition caused him to reject at once the teaching of this school, and he refused to enter it.

His work was interrupted by the war. Mobilized in 1940, he worked as a farmer near Montpellier until 1945.

Once more he returned to painting and settled in Paris in 1946. At this time be began to exhibit first at the Salon des Surindépendants, then at the Salon de Mai in which he has since participated every year. In 1949 he held his first one-man exhibit at the Galerie Lydia Conti in Paris. He next took part in a group exhibit at the Galerie de France in 1951, then in two exhibits at the Galerie Louis Carré in 1952 and 1953. At the same time, numerous individual exhibits were held in Paris and abroad: Birch Gallery, Copenhagen, in 1951; Stangl Gallery, Munich, in 1952; Kootz Gallery, New York, in 1954, 1955, 1956, 1957; Gimpel Fils, London, in 1955; Galerie de France, Paris, in 1957.

In addition, he has taken part in important international artistic events, among them: Venice Biennale, São Paulo Bienal, in the "Younger European Painters" exhibition at The Solomon R. Guggenheim Museum in New York, and in the Carnegie Institute Internationals in Pittsburgh, in the "New Decade" exhibition at The Museum of Modern Art, New York, where he appeared as one of the five painters chosen by the museum to represent France.

Soulages obtained a prize at the São Paulo Bienal in 1953, and in 1957 he was awarded the first Windsor Prize, and the prize of the International Exhibition in Tokyo. He received the Grand Prize at the Biennale de Gravure in Ljubljana, Yugoslavia in 1959.

Soulages has also designed stage sets for a number of plays and ballets, including Graham Greene's *The Power and the Glory*, performed in Paris in 1951.

Several studies and numerous commentaries have been devoted to his work.

Works by Soulages appear in a great number of private collections and museums, among which are Le Musée National d'Art Moderne, Paris; Tate Gallery, London; The Museum of Modern Art, The Solomon R. Guggenheim Museum, Brooklyn Museum, New York; Phillips Collection, Washington, D.C.; Minneapolis Art Museum; Museu Nacional de Belas Artes, Rio de Janeiro; and in Cologne, Hamburg, Essen, Copenhagen, Grenoble, Zurich, Turin, Oslo, and Berlin.

*Plates photographed by Luc Joubert*